# ISIS

*Terrorism and the Rise of Isis*

*Origin of the Islamic State of Iraq and Syria*

**3ʳᵈ Edition**

*CJ Knight*

# ©Copyright 2015 - All rights reserved.

reparation, damages, or monetary loss due to the information herein, either directly or indirectly.

Respective authors own all copyrights not held by the publisher.

The information herein is offered for informational purposes solely, and is universal as so. The presentation of the information is without contract or any type of guarantee assurance.

The trademarks that are used are without any consent, and the publication of the trademark is without permission or backing by the trademark owner. All trademarks and brands within this book are for clarifying purposes only and are the owned by the owners themselves, not affiliated with this document.

**Disclaimer Notice:**

Please note the information contained within this document is for educational and entertainment purposes only. Every attempt has been made to provide accurate, up to date and reliable complete information. No warranties of any kind are expressed or implied. Reader acknowledge that the author is not engaging in the rendering of legal, financial or professional advice.

By reading this document, the reader agrees that under no circumstances are we responsible for any losses, direct or indirect, which are incurred as a result of the use of information contained within this document, including, but not limited to, -- errors, omissions, or inaccuracies.

*CJ Knight*

# Table of Contents

*CJ Knight*

# Introduction

Over the years, people across the globe have witnessed numerous terrorist threats and attacks from various militant groups. Few terrorist activities surface because of failure to analyze the intelligence behind such acts of violence they are often dismissed as a personal feud or as the act of violence by an unstable individual and there ends the interrogation into the roots of their actions. For this reason we have seen an alarming increase and a wider reach of many active terrorist groups.

Al-Qaeda and ISIS began with this kind of perception, but no one ever realized the actual notoriety of the terrorist groups in other countries until the impact hit home. That is the case of the United States of America. It was not essential to know what ISIS was, until the beginning of this year, when active involvement of the U.S troops in the fight against the ISIS began in June, 2014. It has made it important for every American to know whom they are fighting against and for what cause and Americans are searching for answers to what appears to be a violent threat.

Is ISIS just another terrorist group that grabs the attention of the social media for a short while and disappears into nothingness? Or is it an organization that has its roots in violence and branches all over the world? What is their motto? What are their strategies? Who heads them? How should we respond to what we are hearing?

All of these questions are about to meet answers in 'ISIS'.

# Chapter 1

# Origin

Any organization is formed for a purpose. To understand the motives of the ISIS, it is necessary for us to understand the rationale behind the establishment of the organization. Just like any other organization, the ISIS also has undergone many structural changes over the decades. In this chapter, we shall see the growth of the organization from its inception in 1999 until 2014.

## Jamā'at al-Tawhīd wa-al-Jihād

The group was originally formed in 1999 and functioned under the name of Jamā'at al-Tawḥīd wa-al-Jihād ("The Organization of Monotheism and Jihad") (also known as the JTJ). It was founded by Abu Musab al-Zarqawi and a group of Islamist and Jordanian militants.

It was founded with the intention to overthrow the Kingdom of Jordan which, according to Abu Musab al-Zarqawi, functioned against the interests of Sunni Muslims. He went on to enter into numerous contracts and gain affiliates in several countries to achieve their single goal – overthrowing the Kingdom of Jordan.

After the US-led invasion of Afghanistan, al-Zarqawi moved into Iraq and is believed to have developed ties with Ansar al-Islam, a Kurdish Islamic militant group.

In 2003, post the US-led invasion of Iraq, JTJ extended their militant operations to resist the coalition forces occupying Iraq and the Iraqi forces. Their re-stated goals were as follows:

- To force the withdrawal of coalition forces from Iraq

- To overthrow the interim Government set up in Iraq.

- Assassination of the collaborators

- To eliminate the Shia population and defeat its military forces, which were famous for their death squad activities

- Establishment of a pure Islamic state post the evacuation of the coalition forces.

JTJ went on to claim responsibility for a lot of the Iraqi insurgent attacks and attacks against the Iraqi infrastructure. Some of the notable insurgent attacks against Iraq for which JTJ was held responsible are as follows:

| Date | Incident | Casualty Details |
|------|----------|------------------|
| 7th August, 2003 | Bombing of the Jordanian embassy in Baghdad | Killed – 17<br>Injured – 40 |
| 19th August, 2003 | Bombing of the Canal Hotel | Killed – 23 (including Sérgio Vieira de Mello)<br>Injured – More than 100 |
| 29th August, 2003 | Bombing of the Imam Ali Mosque in Najaf | Killed – More than 86<br>Injured – More than 500 |
| 12th November, 2003 | Truck bombing in Nasiriyah | Killed – 27 (10 civilians and 17 Italian paramilitary policemen) |

| | | Injured – 100 |
|---|---|---|
| 2nd March, 2004 | Series of bombings in Karbala and Baghdad on the Day of Ashura | Killed – 178 Injured – at least 500 |
| 18th May, 2004 | Car Bombing assassination | Killed – Ezzedine Salim, President of Iraqi Governing Council |
| 18th June, 2004 | Suicide car bombing in Iraq | Killed – 35 Injured – 145 |
| 14th September, 2004 | Car bombing on Haifa street in Baghdad | Killed – 47 Injured – 100 |
| 30th September, 2004 | Bombing at Baghdad | Killed – 41 |

Apart from these, JTJ claimed credits for attacks against humanitarian aid agencies like the Red Crescent Movement, the International Red Cross and the massacre of the 49 unarmed Iraqi National Guard recruits.

JTJ was also notable for holding many foreign hostages and beheading them. Some of the known foreign hostages are as follows:

- Nick Berg, American civilian

- Murat Yuce, Turkish civilian

- Kim Sun-il, South Korean civilian

- Georgi Lazov, Bulgarian civilian

- Ivaylo Kepov, Bulgarian civilian

- Durmus Kumdereli, Turkish civilian

- Eugene Armstrong, American civilian

- Jack Hensley, American civilian

- Kenneth Bigley, British civilian

## Camp Bucca

The real beginnings of the group known today as ISIS seem to have been traced back to a US Military prison called Camp Bucca. This was the largest US prisons based in Iraq and also one of the toughest and, as insurgency rose dramatically across Iraq, so the numbers at the prison began to swell.

There is significant evidence though that this is the place where ISIS was born. No less than twelve of the top-level leaders of the group served time at the prison, including Abu Bakr al Baghdadi, the man who would eventually take over the group. Nobody could possibly have predicted that he would become possibly the most wanted man in the world. Incarcerated for an unknown crime, Baghdadi was at Camp Bucca for 10 months and, during that time, he would have come into contact with a number of the world's most dangerous Islamic extremists and it is now believed that Camp Bucca is where the initial planning took place.

At the time, US officials working at the camp did voice their concerns that some of the prisoners were becoming "radicalized" and the prison has since been described as a "pressure cooker for extremism". But that was not the only problem there.

Camp Bucca was the place where an extremely powerful and totally unexpected alliance was formed between the Ba'athists who showed loyalty for Sadam Hussein and were bitter at the loss of power they were facing, and the Islamic extremists. The mix became a highly organized discipline, made up of people with a high level of motivation and ideological fervor and the result was, and still is a highly volatile and toxic group.

A rehabilitation program was started in Camp Bucca in an attempt to combat the rising extremism but it was never effectively implemented and, by then, it was too little too late. At this time, Iraq was in chaos and, with 100,000 prisoners and the US focusing all their efforts on the insurgency, there simply wasn't time or the forethought to look at what was really happening and what the future may hold.

*CJ Knight*

# Chapter 2

# Al-Qaeda in Iraq

In October 2004, JTJ pledged its allegiance to Osama Bin Laden and his Al-Qaeda network though a letter and renamed them as the <u>Tanzim Qaidat al-Jihad fi Bilad al-Rafidayn</u>. They were popularly referred to as Al-Qaeda in Iraq (AIQ) later.

## Violent activities

From October 2004, their involvement in insurgent activities against Iraq continued. In the very same month they pledged their allegiance to Al-Qaeda, they were involved in the operation of kidnapping and killing Shosei Koda, a Japanese civilian.

AQI became the main target of the Operation Phantom Fury, led by the US in Fallujah in November. However, AQI managed to escape the American siege with the efficient leadership of al-Zarqawi.

In December, AQI was responsible for bombing a Shia Funeral Procession in Najaf and the bus station situated near Karbala. The death count went above 60.

From 2005 onwards, AQI shifted their focus on the execution of high profile individuals and coordinated suicide attacks. These coordinated suicide attacks were targeted mainly at the administrators of Iraq. Some of the notable insurgent activities during 2005 are as follows:

- Attack on the voters during the Iraqi Legislative election – January, 2005

- Combined conventional and suicide attack on the Abu Ghrahib prison – April, 2005

- Kidnapping and execution of Ihab Al-Sherif, envoy of Egypt to Iraq – July, 2005

- Three day series of suicide attacks and the bombing of the Musayyib marketplace killing at least 150 people – July, 2005

- Single day series of more than a dozen bombings in Baghdad including a bomb attack, which killed around 160 people – September, 2005

- Series of bombings of mosques in the city of Khanaqin, which killed around 74 people – September, 2005

- Coordinated suicide attacks outside the Palestine hotel and Sheraton Ishtar in Baghdad – October, 2005

The year 2006 witnessed an increase in the insurgent activities of the AQI. They claimed responsibility for a lot of major resistance attacks in Iraq.

Some of the incidents that added on to the notoriety factor of AQI during the year of 2006 are as below:

- Capture, torture and beheading of Thomas Lowell Tucker and Kristian Menchaca, two US soldiers.

- Kidnapping and killing of four Russian embassy officials

- Series of crude chemical bombings in Iraq.

2006 was also the year in which several key members of the AQI were killed or captured by American or allied forces. June saw the killing of Al-Zarqawi, Sheik Abd-Al-Rahman and Hamid Juma

Faris Jouri al-Saeedi. Post the death of Al-Zarqawi, the leadership mantle of AQI was passed on to Abu Ayyub al-Masri, an Egyptian militant.

## AQI – ISI – ISIL

Abu Mus'ab al Zarqawi was killed on the 7th June by a US airstrike and, after Masri was named as leader, in October 2006 he announced that the Islamic State of Iraq had been formed and would be led by none other than Abu Umar al Baghdadi. ISI was formed as a way of politicizing the terrorist activities of AQI and to give their efforts an "Iraqi face".

In 2007, AQI continued their reign of terror against the Sunni civilians, attempting to repress them, but this caused a backlash of epic proportions. That backlash was called the Sunni Awakening and resulted in The Awakening Councils being formed, made up of a cross section of local community and tribal leaders. At the same time, AQI was further hampered in their efforts by an increase in Iraqi government and coalition operations that managed to shut down many of their safe havens. This restricted their freedom of movement and, from the middle of 2007, their attacks slowly dwindled.

AQI carried out several high-profile attacks 2009 and 2010. This was meant as a demonstration of the relevance of AQI following the withdrawal of forces from Iraq in 2009. But, it was also meant to position the group to take advantage of the security changes that were taking place in the country. AQI suffered a great setback and loss when Masri and Abu Umar al Baghdadi were killed in April 2010.

The next successor to lead AQI was Abu Bakr al Baghdadi and the high profile attacks continued throughout Iraq, with the group attempting to expand. In the first six months of 2013, around 1000 Iraqi civilians were killed through car bombs and suicide bombers, marking the biggest monthly death toll through violent means since 2008. In April of 2013, Bakr al Baghdadi declared that AQI was now operating inside of Syria and the name was changed to ISIL – Islamic State of Iraq and the Levant.

At the time he announced ISIL, al Baghdadi claimed that AQI was the founder of the al Nusrah front in Syria and that, as of now, the two organizations would be merged. Al Nusrah denied that they were merging and pledged their allegiance to Ayman al Zawahiri, the leader of Al-Qaeda.

AQI took their violence to new highs in august of 2005 when they attempted to launch a rocket attack on a Navy ship that was moored in Jordan, in the Port of Aqaba. That was followed by bombs at three hotels in Amman, leaving over 150 people injured and 67 dead. In 2012, the group leader made halfhearted and vague threats against all Americans, no matter where they were. Before that, an event that highlighted the potential threat was the arrest of two Iraqi refugees with AQI affiliations in May 2011 in Kentucky.

## Mujahedeen Shura Council

The Mujahedeen Shura Council was created by the al-Qaeda in Iraq in January 2006 as an umbrella organization of at least six Sunni extremist jihadist groups. It was established as an attempt to unify all the Sunni insurgents in Iraq. This was also AQI's tactic to regain popularity.

The official announcement of the formation of the group was posted on the Hanin Net, a jihadist website on January 15th, 2006. It was established to resist the efforts of the American and the Iraqi authorities to overthrow the Sunni supporters of the insurgency.

The efforts of the council to enlist Iraqi Sunnis and the secular groups were not so successful because of the violent strategies used by it against the locals and the extreme Islamic Fundamentalist doctrine.

In the month of October 2006, the MSC announced the formation of the Islamic State of Iraq comprising of the six Sunni Arab governorates of Iraq with Abu Omar al-Baghdadi assuming the leadership mantle. He assumed the office of the self-proclaimed state's Emir. Abu Ayyub al-Masri assumed the post of Minister of War. The ISI cabinet comprised of ten cabinet members.

In November 2006, the disbanding of the MSC was announced in favor of the Islamic State of Iraq by Abu Hamza al-Mujahir.

*CJ Knight*

# Chapter 3

# Islamic State of Iraq (ISI)

Despite the fact that Jordan was their place of birth and origin, the newly christened group played a key role in Iraq insurgency. It was reported that fighters from outside countries were many in number and that helped bring an element of surprise in their violence oriented activities.

It was on October 15th, 2006 that ISI was established as a merger of Iraqi insurgent groups comprising of a number of Sunni Arab tribes as well who swore their allegiance to ISI. The ISI planned to seize power in the Western and central areas of the country.

ISI comprised of the original Al Qaeda Organization in the Land of the Two Rivers (AQI) organization, al-Qaeda in Mesopotamia – whose leader was Abu Musab al-Zarqawi, the Mujahedeen

Shura Council in Iraq, and Jund al-Sahhaba (Soldiers of the Prophet's Companions), which was integrated into the ISI. It was the ISI commander who commanded allegiance of all members and not the prominent Al-Qaeda chief.

It wouldn't be wrong to claim that Anbar province was the first stronghold of ISI, which, later on, proceeded to hulk out into ISIS, its current day form. It became frequent news to see a few suicide bombings in Rawa, often targeting police personnel and Christian and Shia civilians. It gained control in areas like Ramadi and Fallujah from where the Iraqi forces had to withdraw due to widespread Sunni protests. Besides Anbar, ISI has also targeted districts like Mosul and Baiji.

Al-Zarqawi received a letter in July 2005 wherein Al-Qaeda's deputy leader Ayman al-Zawahiri sketched out a strategy divided into four stages to expand the Iraq War, which included driving out US military forces from Iraq, establishing an Islamic last word, as caliphate, thereby affecting the secular neighboring countries around the region, and finally leading to the Arab–Israeli conflict.

Its birth is a result of a series of some really interesting events. It was January 2006 when Al-Qaeda joined hands with several Iraqi insurgent groups to form Mujahedeen Shura Council. Brain Fishman claimed this was more than a media display. He was of the opinion that this was an attempt to add some Islamic flavor to the whole plot.

Al-Zarqawi's mistakes were distanced from and the organization got rid of unnecessary and inefficient strategically disastrous errors. Four months later, their guru Al-Zarqawi was killed in a major turn of events.

According to some intelligence obtained by the United States of America, the main objective of ISI was to seize control of the western and central regions of the country and convert it into a Sunni Islamic state. However, by late 2007, the group started losing popular support due to rogue and unaccountable violent attacks on friendly regions thereby causing widespread killing and destruction of public property.

## Islamic State of Iraq and Syria (ISIS)

The civil unrest that began in Syria against the government of Bashar al-Assad in March, 2011 was the main reason behind the ISI entering into Syria.

Abu Bakr al-Baghdadi was instrumental in sending Syrian and Iraqi members of the ISI, who were well experienced in guerrilla warfare, across the borders of Syria. The idea was to establish an organization inside the country.

In April 2013, an audio announcement was released by al-Baghdadi bore the world the news of the establishment of the "Islamic State of Iraq and the Levant" (ISIL) also known as the "Islamic State of Iraq and Syria" and the "Islamic State of Iraq and al-Sham".

## ISIS or ISIL?

In June 2014, ISIS advanced into northern Iraq in a surprise move. Their intentions were to take over the cities in the area, including Mosul, which is the second largest city in the country. As part of their quest to establish an Islamic caliphate, the group made threats to bring an armed confrontation against the regional powers.

There is one thing that is confusing though. These fighters are the people who once bowed down to Al-Qaeda and proclaimed them as the leaders. But now, these people are simply too extreme for the terrorist group and we often see their name in two ways in the media – ISIS and ISIL.

So which one is it? Technically speaking both of these names is correct. ISIS and ISIL are one and the same, the group which appeared in 2003 during the US and coalition attack on Iraq and the same group who was once led by Abu Musab al Zarqawi, killed in 2006 in an airstrike by the Americans.

Before 2012, the group was known as the Islamic State of Iraq (ISI). In 2012, they changed their name to the Islamic State of Iraq and Greater Syria (ISIS). Before they were the Islamic State of Iraq and the Levant (ISIL) but they preferred to show a greater presence by declaring that they owned a much bigger area, hence the change to ISIS. Their ultimate goal was to bring about an Islamic State that was wholly based on Islamic or Sharia law.

ISIS is now under the lead of Abu Bakr al Baghdadi and, having now occupied areas in both Iraq and Syria, are advancing at an alarmingly fast pace towards that goal. Their campaign continues as they head towards Baghdad but, although this advance is a relatively new development, ISIS has been trying to take Shiite territory for many years but has never had the support nor the capacity to succeed.

One strategy that was reported on in 2011 remains very much alive today. Their plan was to incorporate four separate strategies to overcome the US-led coalition present in Baghdad and one of those strategies was to force the US military into joining a Sunni-Shiite civil war. They would do this by targeting the Shiites. In 2014, they announced that they intended to attack Shiite shrines to the south of Baghdad and, although the US said that they would not send their troops into Iraq, they did move an aircraft carrier to the Persian Gulf.

The US withdrew from Iraq in 2011 and since then ISIS has upped the number of attacks made on government bodies in a bid to try to start a fight between Prime Minister Nouri Al Maliki and the Shiite government. The result was the bloodiest year since 2008.

So far though, ISIS has yet to gain any real foothold in Shiite communities, only in a few Sunni areas to the north. And, if the experts are to be believed, the closer ISIS gets to Baghdad, the harder it will become for them. They will first have to gain Shiite support but there is one thing its favor – they have taken control of a mass of heavy weaponry, including tanks and helicopters that were left in Mosul when the Iraq military left. This could tip things their way but only time will tell.

## The Ultimate Goal – Sharia Law for Everyone

The ultimate goal of the Islamic State of Iraq and Syria is just that – one Islamic state where Sharia law would be the only law and freely practiced. In the summer of 2014, al Baghdadi pronounced himself the leader of this Islamic state but, as of yet, it has yet to be given any recognition by any country that has a Muslim majority.

They have gone much further than AQI did by establishing a system of continuous electricity and a consistent court system. That system included punishments for what are seen as violations to Sharia law and consists of beheadings, stoning's, beatings and whippings, depending on the extent of the violation.

ISIS is of the strong belief that they are able to create the perfect society, or what they believe is the perfect society – the one that the Prophet Muhammad established. However, the way that ISIS has gone about this has led to rejection by groups that were previously allies, groups like Al-Qaeda. The rejection is down to condemnation of ISIS for murdering Muslims, as this is not seen as a true reflection of what Muhammad stood for. Instead, it is perceived as a terrible twist, one group's interpretation of what should, in effect, be a peaceful society.

The word Sharia also means Path and is there to guide a Muslim's life – their daily lives, family, religious and financial aspects. It comes from the Quran and the Sunna and was developed several hundred years after the Prophet Muhammad died in 632 CE. His way of life was chosen because he was seen to be the most pious but each school of Islam interprets it differently and some communities follow more than one school of Sharia law.

# Chapter 4

# ISIS-An Insight into Violent Tactics

In this chapter, I will explain the ideology, principles and the various violent tactics of the ISIS.

Ideology

ISIS went on to continue as a Sunni extremist group propagating religious violence and followed an extreme interpretation of Islam.

The ideology of the ISIS can be traced back to the pseudo Islamic Wahabbi ideology that rejects any innovations in the religion. These innovations, according to them, corrupt the spirit of Islam. It adopted the Jihadist principles that were adopted globally.

The concept of using violence to purify the unbelievers in the religion of Islam originates from the Wahabbi ideology. ISIS was a staunch believer of the strict Salafist doctrine where the people who were followers of the secular law were considered as disbelievers.

Goals

Since 2004, the only aim of the ISIS has been the establishment of an Islamic state. The founder and the caliph of the ISIS, Abu Bakr al-Baghdadi, demanded the allegiance of all the devout believers in the religion of Islam.

ISIS now claims provinces and controls several territories in Sinia, Iraq, Syria and eastern Libya.

It also claims provinces and has members in Yemen, Algeria and Saudi Arabia. However, it does not control any territories here.

Governance

As mentioned earlier, the group was headed by Abu Bakr al-Baghdadi along with his cabinet members. Abu Muslim al-Turkmani was the deputy leader responsible for the region of Iraq and Abu Ali al-Anbari was the deputy leader responsible for the region of Syria. Apart from these, they had 12 governors in Syria and Iraq.

Below the governors came the councils on leadership, finance, legal matters and military matters.

The de facto headquarters of the ISIS has been the Ar-Raqqah region in Syria.

As of September 2014, the governance of Ar-Raqqah was totally controlled by ISIL where it has rebuilt the structure of modern government in less than a year. Former government workers from the regime of Bashar al-Assad were allowed to maintain their jobs if they pledged their allegiance to ISIS.

Timeline of events

Post its inception, the ISIS has been involved in a lot of insurgent activities that has shook the reigns of the world in a span of less than two years.

Some of the events that have established the fact that the ISIS members regard violence an end itself instead of as means to an end are as follows:

- Two car bombings in the town of Reyhanli in the province of Hatay, Turkey in which at least 51 people were killed and 140 people were injured – 11th May, 2013

- Killing of Kamal Hamami, the Free Syrian army's battalion chief – July, 2013

- Organized a mass breakout of the members of the ISIS held captive in the Abu Grahib prison, which resulted in the escape of more than 500 members – July, 2013

- The final assault in the siege of Menagh Air base was led by the ISIS – August, 2013

- Killing of Abu Obeida Al-Binnishi, the commander of the Ahrar ash-Sham – September, 2013

- Car bomb attack in the Beirut suburb of Harat Hreik in which four were killed and more than a dozen were wounded – January 2nd 2014.

- Killing of more than a hundred people to take control of Fallujah – January 4th, 2014

- Suicide attack in Aleppo which killed a commander of the Ahrar ash-Sham and 6 members of the group – February 23rd, 2014

- Seven public executions in the city of Ar-Raqqah in northern Syria – May 1st 2014.

- Taking control of the University of Anbar in Ramadi, Iraq and holding around 1300 students as hostage – June 7th, 2014

- Bombing in Jakula that killed 18 members of the Kurdish security forces – June 8th, 2014

Islamic State

The group yet again renamed themselves as the Islamic State on June 29, 2014 claiming itself to be the caliphate with Abu Bakr al-Baghdadi as caliph.

However, this received a lot of criticism from the various Islamic groups across the globe. The declaration of a caliphate has been widely criticized and its legitimacy has been disputed by Middle Eastern governments, Sunni Muslim theologians and historians and other Jihadist groups.

Apart from the objections raised in terms of its ideology, the term "Islamic State" was publicly objected by many for it extends its authority over other countries in terms of religion.

Despite the group renaming themselves, many countries like the United States, Canada, Turkey, Russia, Austria, United Kingdom and the United Nations Security Council continue to refer the group as ISIL or ISIS.

Despite the objections received globally, the ISIS did not put an end to its insurgent activities. After proclaiming itself as the Islamic state, it went to commit well planned massacres and beheadings on a larger scale and the number of casualties has increased in the last few months.

Some of the key events that involved the Islamic state in the last few months are as follows:

- Abduction of 11 civilians from the village of Samra – July 7th, 2014

- Kidnapping of 60 former Iraqi army officials in areas around Mosul – July 9th, 2014

- Massacre of 700 Turkish civilians in the village of Beshir – July 11th and 12th, 2014.

- Execution of 12 men in the village of Tawakkul – July 13th, 2014

- Capturing of 42 Iraqi soldiers in Awenat – July 16th, 2014

- Abduction of 43 Shabak families in the villages near Mosul – July 29th and 30th, 2014.

- Invasion of Lebanon resulting in a five day battle with the Lebanese army – August 2nd, 2014

The month of August, 2014 witnessed the ISIS capture of the Yazidi city of Sinjar and the prompting of the massacre of the inhabitants of the city. By the end of the month, more than 5000 to 7000 Yazidi civilians had been abducted by the ISIS and more than 5000 Yazidi civilians had been killed by them.

## Beheading incidents

The ISIS went on to behead a lot of people and started posting videos of the beheadings to send a message. More than 75 Syrian soldiers were said to have been captured and beheaded during the year. Most of the beheading videos portray the same individual speaking in English who beheads the victims. He is known by the pseudonym "Jihadi John".

Recent beheadings that caught the attention of everyone across the globe was the beheading of the American freelance journalist and photojournalist of the Syrian Civil War, James Wright Foley. He was abducted by the ISIS in November 2012 in the north western part of Syria. He was the first American citizen to have been beheaded by Jihadi John.

Some of the beheading victims of the ISIS include Ali al-Sayyed (a Lebanese Army Sergeant), Steven Joel Soltoff (an Israeli-American journalist), David Haines, Abbas Medlej (a Lebanese army soldier), Hervé Gourdel (French citizen), Alan Henning (a British humanitarian aid worker).

Global response

The beheading incidents received international condemnation. Several political leaders openly voiced their protests against the beheading videos.

# United States of America

The US president, Barrack Obama strongly condemned the violent actions of the militants and Jihadi John and assured that the people behind the videotaped beheadings will be punished before law. John Kerry, the Secretary of the state, called Jihadi John a coward behind a mask.

The White house also released a statement in Twitter that the US strongly condemned the murder of the UK citizen, David Haines when the ISIS released the beheading video of David Haines.

# United Kingdom

The British Prime Minister David Cameron was vocal in expressing his distaste in the murderous activities of the ISIS. He condemned the activities of Jihadi John during his address at the House of Commons the day after the beheading video of Steven Soltoff surfaced.

With more than 500 Britons thought to have travelled to Syria and Iraq with the intention of joining ISIS, the Prime Minister announced that the passports of any who returned to the UK would be confiscated and they would be prosecuted to the full extent of the law.

When the beheading video of David Haines was released, he called it an act of evil in his twitter statement. Although the United Kingdom has send they may send military trainers over to Iraq, they have said that they will not send any troops into combat against ISIS.

## France

Post the murder of journalists James Wright Foley and Steven Soltoff, the Agence France-Presse (AFP) released a statement that it would no longer engage freelance journalists who travel to places, which the AFP would not itself venture.

Hundreds of Muslims gathered in the Grand Mosque of Paris, two days after the beheading of Hervé Gourdel, led by Dalil Boubaker, the leader of the French council of the Muslim faith. The gathering was mainly to express their solidarity against the beheading.

François Hollande, the French president described the act of beheading Hervé Gourdel as cruel and cowardly.

## Germany

The German government has also expressed their intent to provide military supplies and weaponry to Kurdish forces. This follows a previous limitation on the non-lethal aid they were prepared to give but they have not announced any plans to send in personnel.

## Italy

While the Italian government has not committed any troops they are exploring the possibility of being able to send light weapons, i.e. ammunition and guns, to help out the Kurdish forces.

## Syria

When ISIS swept through northern Iraq, they were given a great deal of help from Syria, where extremists were fighting against the opposition in a bid to remove President Bashar al Assad. In a turnabout, ISIS are now overrunning large areas of Syria, parts that were once under the rule of al Assad and the Syrian government has responded with air strikes against the militants.

There was a contention that, in the fight against ISIS, Washington and Damascus would be united against what Syria saw as a common enemy. However, Marie Harf, State Department spokesperson has denied this contention, stating that the Obama administration wants to see al Assad out of the government and no longer in power.

She stated that they did not want to be seen as being on the same page as the regime in Syria, at the same time saying that Syria was in part responsible for allowing ISIS to grow to the extent that it has. The US has also said that they will not rule out any possibility of air strikes in Syria as well as Iraq.

## The Middle East

The Unite States is said to be working in close contact with governments in the Middle East Region, including Jordan, Qatar and Turkey in a bid to cut off sources of private funding for ISIS from civilians who supported their cause.

## Attacks on the Press

Restricting the press has been one of the ancillary goals of the ISIS in the areas controlled by it. Journalists have been brutally captured and killed by the ISIS in the regions controlled by it. In fact, there have been standing orders to kill any journalist that any ISIS soldier might come into contact with.

If the capturing and killing of the journalists was not enough to send a message to the press, the attack on the TV station Salaheddin certainly did enough to startle the Press in the regions which were being controlled by the ISIS. The TV station was accused of portraying the Sunni community of Iraq in the wrong light. Punishment for this blasphemy came in the form of two suicide bombers, who walked into the TV Station in December, 2013 and claimed the lives of five journalists.

Another incident in the month of October, 2014 involved the beheading of a cameraman associated with the TV station Salaheddin. It is believed that nine journalists along with nine other people are still being held as hostages by the ISIS for reasons unknown to the world.

A special division of the ISIS named the Beatles was entrusted with the duty of taking care of the journalists in the areas controlled by it. This unit was responsible for holding close to 12 journalists from the western countries as hostages along with several humanitarian aid workers. From this group of captured journalists, Steven Soltoff and James Foley were beheaded by the ISIS and the videos of their beheadings were posted online by the ISIS to send out a message to their respective countries. Eight journalists have been released so far from the group for ransom. The fates of a female aid worker and the British journalist John Cantlie rest in the hands of the Islamic state as they are still being held as hostages.

The ISIS also went on to claim responsibility for the execution of two journalists from Libya in the month of September, 2014. As recent as January, 2015, a Japanese journalist has been captured and held hostage along with another citizen of Japan and the Islamic State demanded a ransom of two hundred million dollars in return for their safety.

*CJ Knight*

# Chapter 5

# American Reaction to the ISIS

The United States of America has always been the first nation to condemn the activities of the ISIS. The country has gone ahead the extra mile and aided Iraq and Syria in fighting the ISIS.

The two major operations undertaken by the US against the ISIS during the year of 2014 are:

- US-led intervention in Iraq

- US-led intervention in Syria

## US-led intervention in Iraq

The US-led intervention in Iraq commenced when the US President, Barrack Obama, on June 15th 2014, ordered the U.S. forces in Iraq to fight against the militant activities of the ISIS.

Obama ordered the U.S troops to assess the Iraqi forces and the threats posed by the ISIS on the request of the Iraqi Government. The U.S forces started to survey over Baghdad to primarily protect the one hundred and eighty U.S. military advisers who were residing in the area at that point of time.

By the end of the month, the number of U.S troops was increased from 180 to 480 to prevent the ISIS from taking control of the Baghdad International Airport.

Owing to the continuing violence in Iraq and the offensive activities of ISIS, President Obama increased the security commitment in the region. Around 800 U.S troops secured American buildings in the country like the Consulate in Erbil and the Embassy in Baghdad as well as the Baghdad International Airport.

In the month of August, the ISIS organized a Northern Iraq offensive attack and captured the towns of Sinjar, Wana, Zumar on 3rd August 2014. In retaliation to this, the U.S started supplying the Iraqi Kurdis with weapons to fight the ISIS.

## Airstrikes

On 7th August 2014, the U.S President Obama addressed the nation and gave a live statement. He justified the necessity for U.S military action against the ISIS with their increased threats to wipe out the Yazidis, an Islamic minority group in the Northern Iraq. He ordered airstrikes against the ISIS to protect American diplomats, military and civilians in the American Consulate located in Erbil. This was done to stop the potential genocide of the Yazidis by the ISIS.

On 8th August, 2014, the U.S troops bombed the ISIS artillery units, military convoys. A round of airstrikes in the afternoon by the U.S troops struck eight ISIS targets near Erbil.

The purposes of the airstrikes were as follows:

- Protection of the Americans in Iraq

- Helping the Iraqi minorities stranded on the Sinjar region

- Breaking the siege in Sinjar region that had resulted in the stranding of thousands of Yazidis

- Prevention of the genocide of the Yazidis

- Assist the Iraqis in meeting the threats of the ISIS

On 9th August 2014, the U.S forces launched a series of 4 airstrikes against the ISIS fighters, mainly targeting the armored fighting vehicles. The airstrikes were successful in destroying four armored personnel carriers and one unarmored fighting vehicle and killed around sixteen ISIS fighters.

The U.S continued to launch a series of air attacks in the month of August 2014 focusing primarily on the Sinjar region with a view to rescue the Yazidis. Post the mid of August 2014, it started launching air attacks in the region of Mosul Dam to drive the ISIS forces from the region.

In the month of September, the Iraqi government was able to regain the control of the Haditha dam with the continued support of the U.S air force. The U.S air troops continued to aid the Iraqi government and the number of airstrikes continued during the month of September. It launched 11 airstrikes against the ISIS on September 28th 2014.

## Humanitarian aids:

Apart from the airstrikes, the U.S has been extending humanitarian aids to Iraq. In the month of August 2014, the U.S dropped food and water packets to the civilians fleeing the ISIS in the Sinjar region. It dropped thousands of meals and thousands of gallons of drinking water to the Yazidi refugees who were stranded in the Sinjar region.

Apart from these, in the month of November 2014, President Obama had announced the increasing of the U.S troops present on the ground in Iraq.

## US-led intervention in Syria

The United States of America in coalition with five Arab states launched strikes against the ISIS and the affiliates of al-Qaeda in September 2014.

The U.S started sending surveillance drones into Syria to gather intelligence about the various ISIS targets in Syria.

On September 10th, 2014, the U.S President, Barrack Obama declared his intention to bomb the ISIS troops in Syria. He gave his authorization for direct attacks against the militant groups in Syria. He also expressed his intention to train and arm the Syrian rebels to fight against the ISIS.

## Airstrikes

The airstrikes in Syria began on September 22nd 2014. The initial round of airstrikes targeted around 20 ISIS targets. The U.S also targeted the affiliates of al-Qaeda at this juncture. At least 70 ISIS fighters and 50 affiliates of al-Qaeda were killed during the initial round of airstrikes.

As of 19th November 2014, the U.S has been instrumental in carrying out forty six rounds of airstrikes, in coalition with its Arab partners, against the ISIS and al-Qaeda in the region of Syria.

From October 20th 2014, the United States started airdropping supplies to the Syrian Kurdish forces in the region of Kobani. They airdropped weapons, ammunition, medical supplies to the Kurdish forces.

In a statement released by Obama at the White House, he expressed that the strength of the coalition of U.S and the Arab countries made it clear that this was not America's fight alone against the ISIS.

As of 22nd October 2014, the US had spent around $424 million on its bombing campaigns against the ISIS. They have also carried out at least 90 separate airstrikes despite the threats of more beheadings from ISIS.

## ISIS from a Muslim Perspective

There are two schools of thought – one is that all Muslims are a part of ISIS and the second is that Muslims are not speaking out against the atrocities committed by ISIS so they must be a part of it. Neither statement is true and, in fact, it is only a very small majority Muslims who have turned to extremism.

Muslim communities across the world have been speaking out about ISIS and, for the most part, condemning the terrorist acts and the beheadings. In fact, two of the leading Muslim voices have spoken out loudly against ISIS and the persecution of Christians at the hands of the extremists. The loudest voice came from Iyad Ameen Madani. He is the Secretary General for the Organization of Islamic Cooperation, a group that represents 1.4 billion Muslims in 57 countries.

He has denounced that persecution and deportation of Christian as an intolerable crime and has also distanced the Islamic community from ISIS, saying that they are not connected – he says that the principles of the Islamic community were "justice, kindness, fairness, freedom of faith and coexistence".

At the same time, Mehmet Gormez, the top cleric in Turkey and the spiritual successor, under the Ottoman Empire, to the caliphate, also talked about ISIS during a peace conference. His thinly veiled swipe at the group declared that "an entity that lacks legal justification has no authority to declare war against a political gathering, any country or community".

He went on to declare that it is not the way of a Muslim to be hostile towards anyone with a different view from their and who have different beliefs and values and they should not be regarded as an enemy because of it. Gormez also said that the death threats that ISIS make towards those who are not Muslim are incredibly damaging to relations between Muslim and non-Muslim communities.

Muslim leaders across the UK have condemned ISIS and have expressed considerable concern at the level of violence and terrorist acts that are being committed in the name of Islam. Through a video and at a meeting at the Palace of Westminster they repeated their message that ISIS is not representative of the vast majority of Muslims, saying that violence does not have a place in religion.

They are urging Muslims not to join the radical group and said that everybody must be critical, that ISIS is not about establishing an Islamic State; it is about personal gain by a small group. That statement came from the Nahdlatul Ulama, the biggest Islamic organization in the whole world and one that focuses on the traditions of Islam.

These leaders are not the first to denounce ISIS and, indeed, they will not be the last either. The vast majority of Muslims wish to live a peaceful life and do not want to be associated with the most radical terrorist group the world has most likely seen.

*CJ Knight*

# Chapter 6

# Beheading Incidents

The beheading incidents under the regime of the Islamic state have offended the sentiments of countries across the globe and have played an important role in provoking the nations across the globe in coming together to fight against the Islamic state.

In this chapter, the details of the various beheading incidents have been highlighted.

## *Syrian soldiers*

July 25th, 2014 has been an important date which brought out the taste of the Islamic State in terms of beheading. The first victims of beheading by the ISIS included around 75 soldiers belonging to the Syrian Army. These soldiers were captured from an army base and were subsequently beheaded. The photos of the beheadings were posted online by the ISIS. These photos showed the bodies of the Syrian soldiers displayed on the streets.

## James Foley

James Wright Foley was a video reporter as well as American journalist. He was working as a freelance war correspondent when the Civil war in Syria broke out. He was abducted by the ISIS when he was covering the happenings of the Syrian Civil war on the 22nd of November, 2012. He was held as a hostage for almost two years by the ISIS.

Several negotiations happened to rescue Foley from the barbs of the ISIS and the ransom demanded for his freedom was as high as One hundred and thirty two million US dollars. Since his capture, the US intelligence had tried desperately to identify his exact location. However, he was relocated several times by the Islamic State militants making it impossible for the US intelligence to track him and rescue him.

When the United States of America joined the war against the Islamic State by staging air strikes against them in Iraq (more about the air strikes in the later part of this book), the Islamic State beheaded James Foley in the month of August, 2014 and released the video online to send out a message to America. Thus,

James Foley was the first American citizen who was killed by the ISIS. He was beheaded by the infamous "Jihadi John".

## Ali al-Sayyed

Ali al-Sayyed was a sergeant in the Lebanese army. He was captured by the ISIS soldiers during his participation in the battle of Arsal. He was beheaded on August 28th, 2014. The pictures of his beheading were posted on twitter by an ISIS member. This beheading incident was capable of sparking an outrage by the public in Lebanon. The body of Ali al-Sayyed was delivered to the Lebanese authorities four days after he was beheaded.

## Steven Soltoff

Steven Joel Soltoff was a journalist of American-Israeli origin. He was kidnapped on the 4th of August, 2013 when he was crossing the Syrian border along with his family. Though his family members were released fifteen days later, Steven was retained as a hostage.

The news of his kidnapping was not publicized by his family fearing that his life would be at stake. Government agencies combined with efforts of his family worked in secrecy to rescue Steven. His Jewish origin along with his Israeli roots was also kept as a secret fearing that this piece of information would put the life of Soltoff on a higher risk.

When the video of the beheading of James Foley was released, Steven Soltoff was also shown in the video and the ISIS threatened to behead him next if America continued the airstrikes against it in Iraq. Several Americans signed a petition addressing the President to save the life of Soltoff.

However, all the efforts to rescue Soltoff proved futile when the video of his execution was posted online on September 2, 2014 by the ISIS. The beheading video of Steven contained a message to the President of the United States of America, Barack Obama. The message clearly condemned the participation of the US in the attacks against the Islamic State. The beheading of Steven Soltoff was supposedly the Islamic State's response to the US' airstrikes against the Islamic State in the region surrounding the Mosul Dam resulting in heavy casualties for the Islamic State.

## David Haines

David Haines was a British humanitarian aid worker who was working in the refugee camps in Syria. He was kidnapped by an unidentified group of armed people in the March of 2013.

When the news of his kidnapping reached his family, they remained discreet about it based on the instructions issued by the UK Foreign Office as an attempt to rescue Haines safely. However the need to be discreet vanished when David Haines was shown in the video released by the Islamic State that involved the beheading of the American journalist, Steven Soltoff. The British feared that Haines would be the next beheading victim upon seeing this video. The British Prime Minister, David Cameron condemned the acts of Jihadi John and voiced his support to America in its war against the Islamic State.

Attempts to rescue Haines by the American rescue mission were futile because of the continuous relocation of the hostages by the Islamic State.

On September 13, 2014, the video of the beheading of David Haines was released online by the Islamic State. This video was staged similar to that of the previous two beheadings. This video was however addressed to the Allies of America, especially the British Prime Minister, David Cameron. The video condemned the support lent by the British Government to America in their war against the Islamic State and threatened that more deaths would follow should Britain continued to provide its assistance to the United States of America in this regard.

## Abbas Medlej

Abbas Medlej was a soldier in the Lebanese Army. It was believed that the soldiers of the Islamic State captured Abbas Medlej during the Battle of Arsal and held him captive. According to the information released by the Islamic State, Medlej had tried to escape his captors by trying to open fire against them. However, he was overpowered by the alarming number of Islamic State soldiers and was subsequently beheaded. The pictures of his body were posted on several accounts of Twitter which were pro-jihadist in nature.

## Hervé Gourdel

Hervé Gourdel was a citizen of France and was a mountaineering guide. When he was hiking in the Djurdjura National Park in Algeria on September, 2014, he was abducted by the newly formed group ISIS soldiers in Algeria.

The next day, a video of Gourdel being held hostage was released online by an affiliate of the ISIS in Algeria. The video also contained a warning to the French government condemning its involvement in the airstrikes against the Islamic State. It was stated explicitly in the video that Gourdel would be beheaded should the French government continue its aid to the United States of America and launch airstrikes against the Islamic State.

On September 24, 2014, Gourdel was beheaded and the video of his beheading was posted online. This video was filmed on similar lines as that of the previous beheading videos released by the ISIS.

Extensive search by the Algerian soldiers and marines aided by sniffer dogs and helicopters to locate the soldiers of the Islamic State responsible for the murder of Gourdel yielded no results. The death of Gourdel sparked outrage in France and saw thousands of Muslims in France coming forward to voice their contempt against the actions of the Islamic State.

## Alan Henning

Alan Henning was a British humanitarian aid worker. Henning was one of the volunteers who had travelled to Syria in the December of 2013 with the view to deliver food and water to the people affected by the Civil war in Syria.

Henning was supposedly kidnapped by a group of men, who were masked and armed on the 26th of December, 2013. The kidnapping of Henning was unannounced by the British government with an aim to save his life and they negotiated for his safe return discreetly.

Henning was first seen as a captive in the video released by the Islamic State that showed the beheading of David Haines. Jihadi John indicated that Henning would be the next victim if Britain continued its war against the Islamic State.

On October 3rd, 2014, a video was released by the Islamic state online which showed the beheading of Alan Henning. The executioner, Jihadi John, blamed the Britain government for its continued support to the United States of America despite his many warnings.

## Peter Edward Kassig

Peter Edward Kassig, also known as Abdul- Rahman Kassig, was an American citizen. He was a former U.S. Army Ranger. He was working as a humanitarian aid worker in Lebanon and Syria with a view to help Syrian refugees. Having been trained as a medical assistant, Kassig was successful in providing trauma care to many Syrians who were injured in the war and he was also responsible for training many others in terms of providing trauma care.

When Kassig was on his way to deliver food and medicine to the Syrian refugees on the 1st of October, 2013, he was abducted by the ISIS militants. It was believed that he shared the cell with the British journalist, John Cantile and the French journalist, Nicolas Henin. It was also believed that he was beaten on a regular basis. While he was being held captive, Kassig converted to Islam which subsequently resulted in the change of his name to Abdul Rahman Kassig. A video was subsequently released by the parents of Kassig which stated that Kassig's conversion to Islam was not a forced one.

When the video of the beheading of Alan Henning made the rounds in the social media, Kassig was named as the next victim in the video. Several pleas were made by his family addressed to the Islamic State for his safe return. However, these pleas fell into deaf ears when the beheading video of Kassig was released by the Islamic State on November 16, 2014. This video was slightly different from the others as it was not staged like the previous ones. It showed Jihadi John standing over a severed head of a human which was later confirmed to be Kassig. It was believed that Kassig would have fought his captors against reading a written statement and thus the deviation in the style of the video.

In the same video, the beheading of twenty one Syrian soldiers was also shown in blood curdling detail.

## Haruna Yukawa

Haruna Yukawa was a Japanese citizen who aspired to be a private military contractor. During his visit to Syria, he was captured and abducted by the Free Syrian Army in April, 2014. Kenji Goto, a freelance journalist was sent to rescue Yukawa. Both of them returned to Japan. However, Yukawa returned to Syria and he was abducted again in July, 2014. A video was released by the Islamic State in January 2015 which showed Yukawa along with Goto. A ransom of two hundred million US dollars was demanded from the Japanese government for their safe return.

After three days of the release of the video, another video was released online which showed the beheading of Yukawa. Yukawa was thereby the first Japanese citizen to have been killed by the Islamic State.

## Kenji Goto

Kenji Goto was a Japanese freelance video journalist. He was involved in covering conflicts and wars, refugees, AIDS, child education and poverty across the globe.

In the months of September and October, the Islamic State had warned the government of Japan to not return to Syria to aid it during the war. Goto had earlier visited Syria to rescue another Japanese citizen, Haruna Yukawa who was abducted by the Free Syrian Army in April, 2014. He was able to successfully rescue Yukawa and the two of them returned to Japan. Despite these warnings issued by the Islamic State, Goto returned to Syria in October, 2014 to rescue Yukawa again. Goto was however captured by the Islamic State militants on October 25th, 2014.

The beheading video of Kenji Goto was released on January 31st, 2015 making him the second Japanese national who was killed by the Islamic State.

These beheading incidents have been used as a tool by the Islamic State to send messages to various countries who have been fighting against the Islamic state. These have not only succeeded in portraying the Islamic State as a blood thirsty organization but also in invoking terror across the globe.

*CJ Knight*

# Chapter 7

# Life of Women after ISIS

If you were of the opinion that the insurgent activities of the ISIS was a harsh slap across the freedom of people, wait until you know what it means to live under the rule of the Islamic State as a woman! Education and time have served as tools for the development of women. However, with the Islamic state emerging stronger as the days go by, the time turner is back and the lives of women under the rule of the Islamic state have considerably changed. In this chapter, we bring to you the plight of women under the rule of the Islamic State.

## Dress Code

The restrictions on the clothing have raised many eyebrows across the globe! Even conservative Muslims all over the world have been taken aback by the stricter norms imposed by the Islamic State.

According to the protocols issued by the Islamic State, every women living in the regions controlled by the Islamic State ought to remain veiled at all the times. Just wearing a hijab would not do the trick anymore. The Taliban look timid when compared to the Islamic state when it comes to the restrictions imposed on the dress code of women!

Every woman was expected to wear a black abaya which was loose enough so as not to reveal their bodylines. The abaya should also be long enough to cover the entire body. Apart from this, women had to wear a double veil to shield not just their faces but also their eyes from the onlooker. They were expected to wear a shield on the top of their abayas. Moreover, women were allowed to wear only black. That included the shoes and the gloves as well. Anything other than this would be the perfect path for trouble! The religious police of the ISIS, the Hisbah were responsible for overseeing the implementation of the dress code. Any woman found not adhering to the dress code would be rewarded with a good beating to her head by the Hisbah.

If you thought that these applied only for women, then you are wrong. Even girls starting from Class 4th in primary school were expected to wear a hijab at all times. If any girl was sent to the school without the hijab, she would not be admitted into class and would be sent back home.

The atrocities of this stricter dress code do not stop even at times of emergencies. A woman was expected to adhere to the dress code at all times no matter what the emergency might be. It would be appalling to know that even women going into labor are expected to adhere to the dress code. In fact, they would be admitted into the hospital only if they are following the prescribed protocol. Even if a woman was in severe labor pain and if she was not wearing, say a double layered veil, she would be sent back home to wear it and then come to the hospital for treatment. There have been several instances when many women were stopped at the entrance of the hospitals and asked to wear the prescribed clothing if they were keen on getting admitted in the hospital.

More than the household women getting affected by these dress codes, it is the women who go out on a daily basis who are facing the brunt. Be it any profession, women were expected to hide their body and eyes at all times, irrespective of the fact that it might be a hindrance to their jobs. No teacher was allowed to lift the veil inside a classroom, even if it comprised of only girls. Even doctors were not allowed to lift their veils, even if they were treating another female patient. They are expected to perform surgeries with their veils on. If a doctor lifted her veil inside her clinic even if she was alone, the chances of her being reprimanded by the Hisbah are high. Women were allowed to get themselves examined by a male doctor if they were sick. But for no reason are they allowed to lift their veils during the process of examination!

The only people who were exempted from this strict dress code are the women who are over 45 years of age. But then again, it is not an easy ordeal for them either. Often, they would not be admitted into public transports out of the fear that the Hisbah might stop the vehicle and fine the driver for permitting a female passenger who was not adhering to the dress code.

The consequences of not adhering to the dress code are multifold. If a woman was found walking the streets in the areas controlled by the Islamic state, she would have to face one of the following repercussions:

- She would be presented with an Islamic dress along with a pair of black gloves and would be issued a warning not to violate the dress code again.

- She would be taken to the Hisbah headquarters and held their till her mahram came to escort her (more about mahram in the later part of this chapter).

- She would be humiliated in public by the Hisbah with a beating to her head and fined.

It is not just the women who get affected by violating the dress code but their mahrams as well. They either get fined by the Hisbah for permitting the women of their household to violate the dress code or get lashed. The fear of putting the lives of their mahrams in danger mingled with the fear of their dignity getting torn apart has pushed every woman to adhere to the dress code no matter how cumbersome it may be.

The Hisbah patrol the cities controlled by the Islamic State on a daily basis and identify the violators, if any. Apart from this, the Hisbah also stops any form of public transport to look for women who violate the dress code. Suppose, a cab carries a woman who is not adhering to the dress code, then the cab driver would be fined for admitting such a passenger. If a bus was found to carry a passenger who is found to have violated the dress code, all the other passengers would be asked to step down and the bus would not be allowed to proceed any further.

## Restriction on movement

If the dress code rule seemed atrocious, the rules imposed by the Islamic State that restrict the free movement of women are another story altogether. Although these rules seem to be no different from the ones imposed by Taliban in the areas it once controlled.

According to the Islamic State, no woman was allowed to walk the streets unless she is accompanied by her mahram. Mahram is the male guardian of a woman. It can be her husband or brother or father or any male elderly relative who is her guardian.

Women were allowed to leave the houses only at exceptional cases and that too only if they were accompanied by their mahrams. If a woman was spotted walking the streets unaccompanied by her mahram, it is most likely that both the woman and her mahram would be punished by the Hisbah. Fearing this, most women in the regions controlled by the Islamic state hardly step out of their households, let alone the city.

This rule is a nightmare for those households which have no men. The women of such households have no mahram to accompany them anywhere and they can't help but avoid confrontation with the Hisbah for going out of their households unaccompanied. Ideally, if a woman belonging to such a household has to step out to do even a trivial task such as buying groceries for the household, she stands the risk of being reprimanded by the Hisbah.

Just like how the Hisbah check the public transports for identifying the violators of the dress code, they check for women travelling without a mahram. If a woman passenger was found travelling without a mahram, the bus would be stopped and all the passengers would be asked to evacuate and the bus would be sent back for admitting a woman passenger without a mahram.

In most of the regions controlled by the Islamic State, it is not permissible for a woman to be the last passenger while travelling on a bus with just the driver. If all the other passengers get off the bus, then the woman passenger is also made to get off the bus even though it is not her destination.

No woman is allowed to visit the hospital unaccompanied. But the mahram was not permitted to enter inside the clinic. If a man was found inside a clinic by the Hisbah, he would stand the chance of getting arrested by the Hisbah.

## Sexual abuse

Women who were captured by the ISIS would be more than glad to accept the dress code rule and the restrictions on the movement when compared to the amount of the sexual abuse they were made to go through. The plight of the women belonging to the Yazidi community who were captured by the Islamic state militants cannot be explained in words.

The Islamic State militants are told that they had the liberty to kidnap and rape any woman who was not a Muslim. This is perhaps the reason behind the increase in the number of Yazidi women being kidnapped and subject to sexual abuse as you read this book.

The appalling aspect of the sexual abuse is the fact that these women who are captured are traded in the slave market like they were goods. From the group of captured women, usually the older women were sold as slaves in the slave market. On the other hand, younger women and girls were claimed by the soldiers and raped in turns. These girls were apparently the rewards to the soldiers for fighting bravely. Enslaving and raping women belonging to Non-muslim communities were considered as a part of their jihad and the Islamic State views it as a way of purifying the women who are not Muslims.

A documented proof of this horror came in the form of a pamphlet issued by the Islamic State which was circulated to all its soldiers. These pamphlets contained guidelines according to which the soldiers were permitted to claim girls hailing from these Non-Muslim communities and have sex with them. These soldiers were allowed to trade the girls they claimed with the other soldiers so long as they have not impregnated them. In most cases, these girls are traded for sex. The pamphlet made it evident that the ISIS considered it as a birth right to enslave and rape women who were not Muslims.

Reports claim that hundreds of women belonging to the Yazidi community and several minority Christian communities have been captured by the Islamic State and been subject to sexual torture. Continuous rape and systematic abuse have been the only constant in the lives of these women in the last few months. Stories speak of rooms of horror where these women are raped day in and day out. When we say women, it includes young adolescent girls who have been scarred for life. If any woman refused to be abused, she was killed immediately. One of the guidelines stated in the pamphlet issued by the ISIS was the permission given to the soldiers to beat the women slaves to discipline them. The salvation for these women can come only in the form of death.

Thus it is evident that life of a woman under the rule of the Islamic state is a living nightmare and death could only be a well deserved gift to many.

*CJ Knight*

# Chapter 8

# Muslim's Reaction to the ISIS

Sometimes, our misconceptions and preconceived notions get us nowhere. That is true in the case of sensitive issues such as these "jihads" that have been staged by various terrorists over the years. We end up stereotyping a particular sect of people every time a terrorist activity is remotely associated with that sect. That is so true in the case of Muslims as well. In this chapter, we bring to you the sentiments of the Muslims towards the actions of the Islamic State.

## Criticism

The actions of the Islamic State have been condemned by Muslims all over the world, especially theologians and religious scholars. The Islamic State has been justifying all their actions based on the verses of the Qur'an and claims it as a birth right to have started this jihad. However, many Muslim scholars have opposed the interpretation of the Qur'an by the Islamic State.

For instance, the sexual abuse of non- Muslim women have been justified by the ISIS on the basis that the Qur'an permits the enslaving the families of the inferior sect and claiming their women. However, various religious scholars have voiced their protest in this interpretation of the Qur'an by the Islamic State. According to these scholars, a single verse from the Qur'an cannot be interpreted in isolation and used to benefit the motives and justify the actions of the Islamic State. According to them, the Qur'an has to be read in total and the meaning should be derived.

Similarly the concept of jihad perceived by the Islamic State has been severely criticized by many Muslims across the globe. According to the Islamic State, all their fights have always been in the name of Allah. However, their violent actions reflect more on their personal prejudices and are not remotely connected to a holy war. Most of their insurgent activities have no roots whatsoever to a religious war which proves that their actions are anything but a jihad. The recent beheadings are another proof to this. They have beheaded several victims just to spite the nations to which these victims belonged to and not because they were a non- Muslim. These personal feuds have driven most of the violent activities of the Islamic state thus.

Several Muslim scholars and leaders have opined that the ultimate victims of the Islamic State are indeed Muslims themselves as opposed to the people from the other religions. This is because of the way the world looks at Islam as a religion associated with terrorism mainly based on the insurgent activities of the Islamic State. Moreover, the way the Islamic State has interpreted the Qur'an and practice Islam as a religion that propagates violence, terror, murder and torture have also created quite a wave among the other Muslims.

Another act of the ISIS which has been condemned severely by the religious scholars is the concept of slavery. Yet again, the Islamic State owes the concept of slavery to the verses of Qur'an. However, theologians and scholars are of the opinion that the Qur'an indeed opposes enslavement of human race and there have been theories which prove that Islam is a religion that does not propagate slavery. This is again a case of interpretation of the Qur'an gone wrong.

It is evident from the above that the Muslims have been the indirect victims of the activities of the Islamic State. Many people who don't possess the knowledge about the Qur'an or Islam have been lead to believe at the outset that the Islamic State is the face of Islam as a religion. However this is not true as Islam has always been the religion that propagates love as opposed to the barbarism propagated by the Islamic State in the name of Islam.

# Chapter 9

# A Brief History of Muslim Expansionism

While it may be confusing for us to understand why so many radical and seemingly violent groups of Islamic extremists came out of nowhere so suddenly within the past twenty years, it honestly hasn't been so hidden. What I have compiled her is a brief history of the expansion of Islam and why it has been such a powerful tool in motivating those across the world who have joined in their causes to expand and carve out a kingdom of theocratic dominance in a world that is seemingly secularized more and more with each passing day.

The tenants of Islamic expansionism have their roots back to when the religion was first founded and established by

Mohammed. Like the Christian Bible, there are accounts in the texts of the Quran that beseech the followers of the faith to take up arms and to eliminate their followers. The discernable difference is that the Christian Bible is divided into two testaments, a New and an Old Testament. The New Testament is the tale of a Christ figure who preaches peace and brotherly love, canceling out the violent nature of the Old Testament. This however, has not stopped Christian forces from utilizing the negative and violent demands of the Old Testament to spread blood. However, the Quran has no discernable separation between the Surrahs. There is no Christ figure or Messiah who preaches peace to curb the violence of men. For the Islamic faith, violence is to be a means of conversion and a tool to establish Islam as the defining faith of the world.

Now, while not all Muslims believe this, it has certainly given those who do believe in it a greater cause and ability to rally those to their banner and war cry. When nations rally under the banner of an Islamic nation or kingdom, it is a declaration that their kingdom is now a theocracy. This means that Allah is in charge of their nation and that Allah has dictated a hierarchy of leadership, ie those currently in charge. This opens up their theocracy to be rife with corruption and the deception that many nations have had trouble with as well.

So, from the declaration of Mohammed's faith, there have been six declared caliphates, which is what ISIS currently believes itself to be. So we'll have a brief look at the most prominent and historically significant of these caliphates and see why they rose to power and how they fell. Remember, these are just the caliphates declared. Islamic forces have declared nations, emirates, sultanates, khanates, republics, and various other kingdoms over the years. But we'll just stick to the caliphates because ISIS very intentionally declared themselves a caliphate for a reason. Keep in mind that these are the standards that ISIS is seeking to reach when they declare their war on the world.

## The Rushidun Caliphate

This is the king of all caliphates and was the nation that started the Islamic theocracies that would follow all across the world. It all began with the death of Mohammed in the year 632 AD and with his sons, the rise of their nation began. Its capital started in the holy city of Medina that was taken by Mohammed during his life and was declared the capital of the Caliphate until it moved to Kufa over twenty years later. What Mohammed's sons did is something just short of military genius that would forever shape the world. The influence of Islam across the globe is traced back to the Rusidun Caliphate and is exactly what ISIS is currently seeking to accomplish.

Mohammed's sons marched their armies all across the Arabian peninsula, bringing stability and order to the lawless and warring tribes of Bedouin peoples that inhabited the area. This was something never seen by the people of these lands and was welcomed with open arms. This expansionist mentality was embraced and given to those tribes that joined willingly or surrendered. Once the Arabian Peninsula was conquered, the Caliphate declared war on the Byzantine Empire, the remnant of the once great Roman Empire, and the Persian Empire, a shadow of the Persian people that were. They expanded north into Turkey, the Levant, and Egypt. At its height, the Caliphate held its dominion over the entire Middle East and was pushing toward central Asia. They conquered all of Turkey and were knocking at the doors of Europe while their dominion crept across Egypt and most of North Africa. The Rushidun Caliphate was also the first Islamic force to push into the Iberian Peninsula and declare war on Spain that would cause civil war on that Peninsula for centuries to come.

The Rushidun Caliphate understood that fair treatment of those that were not of the Islamic faith was necessary to maintain order. If they started killing the Jews, Zoroastrians, and Christians they conquered like ISIS is currently doing, they knew that they could not maintain control. This is a lesson that ISIS has yet to learn. However, it was not enough to maintain power as is.

Like many nations and empires before them, the Rushidun Caliphate's demise is attributed to infighting and assassination that ultimately destabilized the presence of the Caliph. Their demise fractured the known Caliphate into a dozen different nations that would war against each other for centuries over everything form religious differences, to political power, and resources. It was not an invading force that brought the Rushidun Caliphate to its knees, but the people within and the general decay of the nation that they built.

## The Mamluk Caliphate

This refers to numerous nations that rose and transitioned through the Middle East, starting as far back as 1077. As one Mamluk nation fell, it crashed into the rise of another and is enduringly known as the period of the Mamluk Caliphate which was a response to Christian barbarism focused around Jerusalem and the rise of the Papal push for violent Christians to take their bloodlust out on the Muslim nations of the world.

The height of the Mamluk period was with the rise of Egypt under the banner of Saladin who would famously push the Christians Kingdoms out of the Holy Land and would bring Jerusalem back under Islamic command since the First Crusade. The Mamluk Caliphate was not just the target of Christian wrath, but also the wrath of neighboring and warring Islamic nations. Unification was the rise of this Caliphate's strength, something that the current ISIS nation is seeking to unify. Like ISIS the Mamluk Caliphate drew a lot of its strength from the generally reviled and despised presence of Christians or the Christian nations that sought to overthrow and occupy the Middle East. This was a great asset and a tool that they implemented in their unification process until they were strong enough to launch and assault against the Crusader States themselves and throw the majority of the Christians back into the sea.

Like the Rushidun Caliphate, the Mamluk Caliphate descended into anarchy and infighting the moment Saladin died and the transition of power was up for grabs. This led to the Caliphate fracturing and splitting in several places with new Islamic nations spawning out of the limbs of the Caliphate. It wasn't until the arrival of the Mongol Empire that the Mamluk Caliphate traditionally fell and the Mamluks that remained were just a pale shadow of what once was from this once mighty Caliphate.

## The Ottoman Caliphate

What started out as the Ottoman Caliphate quickly turned into the Ottoman Empire or Sultanate by the established European nations. The rapidly growing and powerful nation spawned from Constantinople or Istanbul and once again, started out by uniting the warring Islamic tribes and nations that had descended into infighting, anarchy, and betrayal for centuries. The Islamic world had all but collapsed by the time the Ottomans rose to power. Historically speaking, the Ottoman Caliphate is the most recent success story of Islamic Caliphates to date, enduring all the way until after World War I.

After taking Constantinople, the Ottomans conquered any profitable land held by Islamic people and solidified the region through tolerance, peace, and the united drive to compete and fight against Europe, specifically the Russians and the Greeks. They allied with anyone who would join with them in maintain their lands and the power they held. They served as a major force in global conflicts for hundreds of years, even into World War I where the famed Lawrence of Arabia helped to tear Saudia Arabia away from them.

At their height, the Ottoman Empire had a legacy of military power that was unrivaled by any of the previous Caliphates or any of the other Islamic kingdoms up to that point. They were so powerful that any war that the Ottomans entered was going to be a violent affair where thousands of soldiers could be expected to engage in single battles. They also had a massive battlefront that practically wrapped around their entire nation. If they weren't fighting against Europeans to the north, it was rebels to the east and Islamic tribalism to the south. All around, they were besieged by constant war, yet they endured for centuries. As far as the length of time goes, the Ottomans were the enduring champions of Islamic nations.

What makes the Ottoman Caliphate such a warning sign to a group like ISIS is that the Ottomans knew that militaristic and fanatical Islam was a relic of the past, just like fanatical Christianity. Tolerance, diplomacy, trade, and alliances were needed for a modern nation to survive, especially if they were to be at odds with the Christian nations and kingdoms that existed. ISIS currently has none of these things going for it. They have no tolerance, no diplomacy, no trade, and no alliances of any substantial use to them. Boko Haram and Al-Shabaab are not credible allies of any kind for Isis. Only by actually becoming part of the world could they actually be a substantial presence in the modern, global existence of those around them.

## The Heritage Endures

With most invading and conquering forces in the world, there is always a heritage or legacy that is being idolized and idealized by those of the current nation. For ISIS, they're looking back at the legacy days when the Rushidun Caliphate ruled the entire, known Islamic world and was a force of extreme fear and power. Not only did they have a united empire, but they also carved a path into Europe and actually struck ground against those that would oppose them. However, their legacy also comes with some flaws and some faults that ISIS will have to work extremely hard against seemingly impossible odds if they want to endure. They will have to beat infighting and religious differences that have plagued every Islamic nation to exist to this point, or any theocracy for that matter. They will also have to adopt a semblance of tolerance or they will continue to draw enemies and alienate themselves from those who would ever even consider them allies. Tolerance is the key to managing a population without deeming them as second-class citizens or persecuting them. This will only lead to uprising and betrayal in any lands that ISIS dares to claim as their own. The next key that they will have to understand is that an economy must be established that is not built upon the backs of other economies. They will have to bring something to the table that will require those around them to see their supposed nation as something that is vital and necessary to the stability of the region. Currently, they hold nothing of significant value that could motivate others to see them as a threat. Finally, they're going to have to address the issue that enduring theocracies are rampant with political corruption and military coupes. Being able to stabilize themselves to endure is going to be a long and tough road for them to establish.

Until ISIS can rectify or address these problems that other, greater Caliphates have fallen from, they don't stand a chance.

Already, you can see that they are failing in these crucial moments to establish themselves as an enduring, credible threat to the world outside of being a thuggish terrorist organization.

# Conclusion

Thank you for reading!

I hope that the information provided in this book has helped you understand the functioning of the ISIS. Understanding their motives and their ploys is the first step in combating their efforts. Lack of awareness can be a dangerous thing at this point of time when the United States of America has declared an open war against the terrorist activities of the ISIS.

I sincerely hope that the book was useful in throwing some light over the terrorist organization, ISIS.

Stay alert, stay safe!